Contents

Appendices 132

Introduction

In the vast and ever-evolving digital expanse, the art of web development emerges as a powerful conduit of creativity and innovation. As the virtual realm intertwines more deeply with our daily lives, the ability to craft captivating and functional web experiences transcends being a mere skill; it transforms into a superpower that empowers individuals and organizations alike to connect, communicate, and create in ways that were once unimaginable.

Welcome to the World of Web Development

Welcome, intrepid voyagers, to a transformative odyssey that will peel back the layers of mystery in this dynamic landscape. As you embark on this journey, envision yourself as a modern-day architect, crafting the very foundations of the digital world. From the simplest personal websites to the intricate web applications that underpin our interconnected society, the art of web development has evolved into an essential language of expression.

The web has become a sprawling canvas upon which ideas, businesses, and communities flourish. It's a space where your imagination can run wild, and every line of code you write has the potential to shape how people experience and interact with the online universe. This journey isn't just about learning syntax and techniques; it's about understanding the transformative role you can play in this digital renaissance.

The Importance of HTML and CSS

At the core of this digital tapestry stand two essential pillars: HTML (HyperText Markup Language) and CSS (Cascading Style Sheets). Think of HTML as the architect's blueprint, shaping the structure and content of the digital landscape. It breathes life into the headings, paragraphs, images, links, and interactive elements that populate web pages, transforming lines of code into meaningful content that users can see and engage with.

CSS, on the other hand, dons the mantle of an artist. It's the palette of colors, the brush strokes of typography, and the intricate patterns that turn the blueprint into a visual masterpiece. With CSS, you wield the power to orchestrate a symphony of design, crafting not just functional interfaces but immersive experiences that captivate the senses.

The combination of HTML and CSS is akin to constructing a building. HTML lays the foundation, defining the structure and layout of rooms, while CSS adds the finishing touches—painting the walls, arranging furniture, and adorning the spaces with artistry.

Setting the Stage for Your Learning Journey

As we embark on this grand voyage into the realm of web development, let's take a moment to set the stage for the epic journey that lies ahead. Imagine this journey as a tapestry of exploration, each thread representing a concept learned, each chapter a new hue of knowledge woven together to create a vivid picture of expertise.

The chapters that follow will act as your compass, guiding you through the labyrinthine corridors of web development. You'll navigate the intricacies of tags and attributes, unlock the power of selectors and properties, and delve into the artistry of layouts and interactivity. Think of each lesson as a step toward unveiling the mysteries of the digital realm, a journey of self-discovery and skill acquisition.

And remember, as you embark on this voyage, that every piece of code you write is a brushstroke on the canvas of the web. With each stroke, you're not only gaining knowledge but also asserting your presence in the digital world. So, gather your courage, open your mind to the limitless possibilities, and let's set sail on a journey that will empower you to shape the web with your unique creativity.

The chapters that lie ahead are your stepping stones into the world of web development. They'll empower you with the skills and knowledge to mold your ideas into tangible digital realities. You'll uncover the intricacies of code and design, cultivating a deep understanding of how web pages come to life and how interactions unfold on the virtual stage.

Picture yourself as an explorer, armed with the tools of HTML and CSS, venturing into uncharted territories. Each concept you grasp is a landmark on your map of expertise, guiding you toward becoming a master of the craft. Through the pages that follow, you'll experience the thrill of translating your creative visions into functional websites that resonate with users around the globe.

This journey isn't just about mastering code; it's about crafting experiences that evoke emotions, solve problems, and inspire action. As you navigate the chapters, don't hesitate to experiment, ask questions, and embrace challenges. Remember that every roadblock you overcome is a testament to your growth as a web developer.

Embarking on a Digital Odyssey

Imagine your journey through this book as a digital odyssey. With each page you turn, you're not just absorbing information—you're embarking on an adventure of exploration and creation. As you immerse yourself in the world of web development, you're acquiring a skill set that has the power to shape the digital landscape for years to come.

So, as you dive into the upcoming chapters, let curiosity be your compass and creativity be your guiding star. From the foundations of HTML to the artistry of CSS, you're arming yourself with tools that will allow you to craft digital experiences that transcend boundaries and captivate imaginations.

Ultimately, this journey isn't just about the web—it's about your journey as a learner, an explorer, and a creator. It's about the evolution of your skills and the realization of your potential in a world where the digital realm knows no bounds. So, take a deep breath, gather your enthusiasm, and let's begin this odyssey that promises not just knowledge, but the empowerment to shape the very fabric of the web itself.

Chapter 1: Understanding the Basics

1.1 What is the Web?

Welcome to the captivating realm of web development! Before we dive headfirst into the world of HTML and CSS, it's important to establish a solid foundation by understanding the very essence of the web itself. The internet, a cornerstone of modern life, connects people, businesses, and information across the globe. And at its core, lying like a vast interconnected tapestry, is the World Wide Web.

Imagine the web as a virtual realm where documents, images, videos, and various digital resources come together in an intricate web of connections. This interconnectedness gives rise to an online space that transcends physical boundaries, allowing you to explore, learn, communicate, and even create.

1.2 How Do Websites Work?

As you embark on your journey into web development, it's crucial to grasp the underlying mechanics of how websites function. Imagine typing a URL into your web browser's address bar—a seemingly simple action that initiates a fascinating chain of events.

Behind the scenes, a web server receives your request and promptly responds by sending back the requested web page's files—these files include HTML, CSS, and often JavaScript. Your browser then takes on the role of an artist, meticulously assembling these files to create the visual masterpiece you see on your screen.

HTML (HyperText Markup Language) serves as the building blocks, providing the structure and content of the page. You can think of HTML as the scaffolding that holds everything together. CSS (Cascading Style Sheets), on the other hand, steps in as the painter, applying colors, fonts, spacing, and layout, transforming the raw structure into an aesthetically pleasing, user-friendly design. And finally, JavaScript, the magician of interactivity, adds dynamic behavior, turning static pages into engaging experiences.

1.3 Introduction to HTML and CSS

Now, let's turn our focus to HTML and CSS—the dynamic duo that empowers you to shape the digital landscape. HTML, often hailed as the backbone of the web, is a markup language that uses a system of "tags" to define the elements and layout of content within a web page.

Imagine HTML as a set of blueprints for a house. Each tag serves a distinct purpose: headings define the importance of text, paragraphs provide structure to content, images add visual context, and links connect the web together. By combining these tags, you orchestrate the symphony of information that your users experience.

On the other hand, CSS steps onto the stage as the artist's palette. Cascading Style Sheets allow you to wield creative control over the presentation of your web page. You can alter colors, adjust fonts, arrange content with precision, and create a visually cohesive design. Think of CSS as the paint that adds depth, beauty, and character to the canvas of your HTML structure.

1.4 Tools and Resources You'll Need

Now that we've set the stage, you might be wondering, "How do I begin my journey in web development?" The answer lies in equipping yourself with the right tools and resources. Just as a craftsman needs a toolkit, a web developer needs a set of digital tools to bring their ideas to life.

First on your list is a text editor—a digital notepad where you'll craft your code. Text editors come in various flavors,

from the simplicity of Notepad to the feature-rich
powerhouses like Visual Studio Code. These editors provide
an environment where you can write and organize your
code efficiently.

Of course, what's a web developer without a trusty web
browser? Your browser serves as both a canvas and a
testing ground. You'll use it to preview and interact with
the web pages you create. Popular choices include Google
Chrome, Mozilla Firefox, and Microsoft Edge.

For those seeking an enhanced coding experience, an
integrated development environment (IDE) might be your
cup of tea. IDEs offer a comprehensive workspace with
advanced features like code suggestions, debugging tools,
and project management capabilities.

And last but certainly not least, the web development
community is here to support you. A wealth of online
resources awaits—tutorials, documentation, forums, and
vibrant communities of fellow learners and seasoned
developers. Whenever you encounter a challenge,
remember that you're not alone in your quest for
knowledge.

With these tools at your disposal, you're ready to step into
the world of web development. The journey ahead is filled

with exploration, learning, and the joy of bringing your creative visions to life through HTML and CSS.

Chapter 2: HTML Fundamentals

Welcome to the immersive world of HTML, where you'll learn to create the structural foundation of web pages. In this chapter, we'll delve deep into the core elements of HTML that lay the groundwork for crafting dynamic and engaging digital content. By the end of this journey, you'll be empowered to construct web pages enriched with headings, paragraphs, links, and images—a web of information that's both functional and visually appealing.

2.1 Structure of an HTML Document

To understand the architecture of a web page, let's imagine it as a digital canvas awaiting the brushstrokes of content. Much like a painter starts with a canvas, you'll begin with an HTML document—a framework that instructs web browsers how to render your content. This document consists of a structured sequence of elements, each playing a specific role in defining the layout and display of your web page.

At the heart of every HTML document is the <!DOCTYPE> declaration. This line informs the browser about the version of HTML you're using. It's like setting the stage for a play, ensuring that all actors follow the same script. After the <!DOCTYPE>, you have the root element, <html>, which serves as the container for all other elements in the document.

The <html> element encloses two main sections: <head> and <body>. The <head> section contains metadata about the document, such as character encoding and the title displayed in the browser tab. It's where you provide essential information to browsers and search engines.

```html
<!DOCTYPE html>

<html>

<head>

   <meta charset="UTF-8">

   <title>My Web Page</title>

</head>

<body>

   <!-- Your content goes here -->

</body>

</html>
```

The <body> section houses the visible content of your web page, where you'll weave together the textual and visual elements that users interact with. This separation between <head> and <body> ensures that browsers process your document efficiently and display it accurately to visitors.

2.2 Creating Headings and Paragraphs

Imagine your web page as a story waiting to be told. Headings and paragraphs are the storytelling elements that guide your readers through the narrative. Headings establish a hierarchy of importance, creating a roadmap that helps users navigate your content. HTML offers six levels of headings, from <h1> (the highest level) to <h6> (the lowest). Each heading level represents a different chapter in your story, with <h1> introducing the main theme and <h6> addressing minor details.

```
<h1>Welcome to My Website</h1>
<h2>About Me</h2>
<h3>Education</h3>
```

On the other hand, paragraphs provide structure to your text. When content is presented in large, unbroken blocks, it can be overwhelming for readers. Paragraphs break up the information into digestible portions, making it easier for users to process and comprehend your message.

```
<p>Lorem ipsum dolor sit amet, consectetur adipiscing elit...</p>

<p>Ut enim ad minim veniam, quis nostrud exercitation ullamco...</p>
```

Effective use of headings and paragraphs transforms your content into an engaging and coherent narrative, guiding readers through your web page with clarity.

2.3 Working with Links and Anchors

In the interconnected web landscape, links are the bridges that connect users to various destinations. The <a> (anchor) element is your tool for creating these links. The most basic use of the <a> element involves the href attribute, which specifies the URL where the link will lead.

For external links, you provide the complete URL:

```
<a href="https://www.example.com">Visit Example Website</a>
```

However, you can also link to other pages within your own website by using relative paths:

```
<a href="/about.html">Learn More About Us</a>
```

Anchors aren't limited to text alone. They can also encompass images, buttons, and other interactive elements. For instance, you can transform an image into a link that takes users to another page:

```
<a href="destination.html">

  <img src="image.jpg" alt="Click me for more details">

</a>
```

This versatility in linking provides users with intuitive navigation, allowing them to explore and engage with your content seamlessly.

2.4 Adding Images to Your Web Page

Pictures speak volumes, and in the digital realm, images play a crucial role in enhancing user experience. The <img> element empowers you to seamlessly integrate images into your web pages, adding depth and visual appeal to your content. By utilizing the src and alt attributes, you can control both the display of the image and its accessibility for users with disabilities.

```
<img src="image.jpg" alt="A beautiful landscape">
```

The src attribute points to the image file's location, allowing the browser to retrieve and display the image. Meanwhile, the alt attribute provides alternative text that is displayed if the image cannot be loaded. This not only ensures that users with visual impairments can understand the content but also helps improve your website's search engine optimization (SEO).

Images are far from mere decorations—they communicate emotions, add context, and infuse life into your web pages. A carefully chosen image can captivate users, encouraging them to explore further.

Congratulations! You've embarked on a journey to master the art of HTML. By grasping the structure of an HTML document, creating meaningful headings and paragraphs, seamlessly linking content, and integrating captivating images, you've gained essential skills for crafting well-rounded web pages. But this is just the beginning. In the upcoming chapters, we'll explore the diverse array of HTML elements and tags that empower you to create even more interactive, dynamic, and visually engaging content.

So, continue your exploration with a sense of wonder and curiosity. HTML is the canvas, and each element you master is a stroke of creativity that shapes your digital masterpiece.

In Chapter 3, we'll dive deeper into the world of HTML by exploring a wider range of elements, from lists to forms, that enable you to craft diverse and interactive content.

This concludes the second part of the expanded Chapter 2. If you have any specific points you'd like to add or explore further, feel free to let me know.

Chapter 3: HTML Elements and Tags

In Chapter 2, you uncovered the foundational elements of HTML, from the structural framework of an HTML document to the power of headings, paragraphs, links, and images. Now, it's time to expand your HTML repertoire as we dive deeper into the diverse world of HTML elements and tags. These elements serve as the building blocks that transform your web pages from static documents to interactive and dynamic experiences.

3.1 Text Formatting with HTML Tags

Text on a web page is more than just words—it's a means of communication that conveys information, emotion, and style. HTML offers a range of tags that allow you to format your text and make it visually appealing.

Bold and Italic Text

The <b> and <i> tags are two fundamental tools for text emphasis. The <b> tag represents bold text, making the enclosed content stand out with a thicker and darker appearance. On the other hand, the <i> tag is used for italicized text, creating a slanted effect that can add emphasis or convey a different tone.

```
<p>This is <b>bold</b> and <i>italic</i> text.</p>
```

Underlined and Strikethrough Text

Sometimes, you might want to draw attention to specific text using underlining or indicate deleted content with a strikethrough. The <u> tag creates underlined text, while the <s> tag adds a strikethrough effect.

```
<p>This is <u>underlined</u> and <s>strikethrough</s>
text.</p>
```

Superscript and Subscript Text

HTML also offers the <sup> and <sub> tags to display text as superscript (raised above the baseline) or subscript (lowered below the baseline). These tags are commonly used for mathematical notations, footnotes, and chemical formulas.

```
<p>H<sub>2</sub>O is the chemical formula for water.
E=mc<sup>2</sup> is Einstein's equation.</p>
```

Line Breaks and Horizontal Rules

To control the line breaks and spacing within your text, you can use the <br> tag. This tag creates a simple line break without adding extra spacing. If you're looking to create a visible separation between sections, the <hr> tag inserts a horizontal rule—a thematic divider that spans the width of its container.

```
<p>This text<br>has a line break.</p>

<hr>
<p>Sections are divided by a horizontal rule.</p>
```

By wielding these text formatting tags, you can imbue your content with emphasis, structure, and clarity, enhancing the readability and impact of your web page.

In the next part of Chapter 3, we'll explore the art of creating lists using HTML, providing you with the tools to organize information in a concise and visually appealing manner. Stay tuned for an exploration of ordered lists, unordered lists, and definition lists, each serving a unique purpose in presenting content.

3.2 Creating Lists: Ordered, Unordered, and Definition

Imagine reading a web page without any organized structure—it would be like navigating a maze with no clear path. Lists are the navigational signposts of your content, guiding readers through information in an organized and coherent manner. HTML offers three main types of lists: ordered lists, unordered lists, and definition lists.

Ordered Lists

Ordered lists are used when you want to present items in a specific sequence or order of importance. Each item is preceded by a number or letter, indicating its position in the list.

```
<ol>

  <li>Wake up</li>

  <li>Brush teeth</li>

  <li>Eat breakfast</li>

</ol>
```

Unordered Lists

Unordered lists, on the other hand, present items without
a strict sequence. Bullets or other symbols are used to
mark each item.

```
<ul>

  <li>Apples</li>

  <li>Bananas</li>

  <li>Oranges</li>

</ul>
```

Definition Lists

Definition lists are a powerful tool for presenting terms and
their corresponding definitions. Each term is enclosed
within a <dt> (definition term) tag, while its definition is
enclosed within a <dd> (definition description) tag.

```
<dl>

  <dt>HTML</dt>

  <dd>Hypertext Markup Language</dd>

  <dt>CSS</dt>

  <dd>Cascading Style Sheets</dd>

</dl>
```

Nested Lists

You can also nest lists within one another to create more complex structures. For instance, you might use an ordered list as the outer list and an unordered list as its nested inner list.

```
<ol>

  <li>Introduction</li>

  <li>Main Content

    <ul>

      <li>Section 1</li>

      <li>Section 2</li>

    </ul>

  </li>
```

```
<li>Conclusion</li>
</ol>
```

By skillfully utilizing these list types and their variations, you'll be able to organize content, present information hierarchies, and make your web pages more reader-friendly and visually engaging.

In the next part of Chapter 3, we'll venture into the realm of tables—a powerful HTML tool for displaying structured data. You'll discover how to create tables, populate them with data, and customize their appearance using CSS. Tables are the gateway to presenting information in a tabular format, and your mastery of this skill will elevate your web pages to new heights of functionality.

Stay tuned for the exciting exploration of tables in the next section!

3.3 Building Tables for Data

Tables are a cornerstone of presenting structured data on the web. Whether you're displaying sales figures, comparison charts, or any form of organized information, tables provide a systematic and organized layout. HTML empowers you to create tables with rows and columns, and with the right styling, you can make your tables not only informative but visually appealing as well.

Creating a Basic Table Structure

At the heart of every table is the <table> element. Within this element, you define rows using the <tr> (table row) tag, and within each row, you define cells using the <td> (table data) tag.

```
<table>
  <tr>
    <td>John</td>
    <td>Doe</td>
    <td>25</td>
  </tr>
  <tr>
    <td>Jane</td>
    <td>Smith</td>
    <td>30</td>
  </tr>
</table>
```

Table Headers

For better clarity and structure, you can use the <th> (table header) tag to define header cells for columns and rows. These cells are typically bold and centered, helping readers quickly identify the content of each column or row.

```
<table>
  <tr>
    <th>First Name</th>
    <th>Last Name</th>
    <th>Age</th>
  </tr>
  <tr>
    <td>John</td>
    <td>Doe</td>
    <td>25</td>
  </tr>
  <tr>
    <td>Jane</td>
    <td>Smith</td>
    <td>30</td>
  </tr>
```

```
</table>
```

Cell Alignment and Spanning

You can control the alignment of cells within a table using the align attribute. Additionally, you can use the colspan attribute to make a cell span multiple columns or the rowspan attribute to make a cell span multiple rows.

```
<table>

  <tr>

    <th>Header 1</th>

    <th colspan="2">Header 2</th>

  </tr>

  <tr>

    <td>Cell 1</td>

    <td>Cell 2</td>

    <td>Cell 3</td>

  </tr>

  <tr>

    <td rowspan="2">Spanned</td>

    <td>Cell 4</td>

    <td>Cell 5</td>
```

```
  </tr>

  <tr>

    <td>Cell 6</td>

    <td>Cell 7</td>

  </tr>

</table>
```

Styling Tables with CSS

While HTML provides the structure of tables, CSS enables you to style them according to your design. You can apply background colors, borders, spacing, and more to achieve the desired visual effect.

```
<style>

  table {

    border-collapse: collapse;

    width: 100%;

    border: 1px solid #ddd;

  }

  th, td {

    border: 1px solid #ddd;

    padding: 8px;
```

```css
    text-align: left;

  }

  th {

    background-color: #f2f2f2;

  }
</style>
```

By mastering the art of building tables, you'll be equipped to present data in a structured and organized manner, enhancing user experience and making your web pages valuable sources of information.

In the next part of Chapter 3, we'll explore HTML forms—a gateway to interactivity and user input on your web pages. Forms are vital tools for gathering information, processing user data, and creating engaging user experiences. Get ready to delve into the world of form elements, input fields, and more!

3.4 Using Forms to Gather User Input

Web pages have evolved beyond being one-way streets of information delivery. With the introduction of HTML forms, your web pages can now become dynamic platforms for interaction, user input, and data collection. Forms enable you to create a wide range of user experiences, from simple search bars to complex registration processes.

Form Structure

At the core of every HTML form is the <form> element. This element serves as a container for various input elements that allow users to provide information. The action attribute specifies where the form data should be sent for processing, and the method attribute defines how the data should be transmitted.

```html
<form action="process.php" method="post">

  <!-- Form input elements go here -->

</form>
```

Text Input Fields

Text input fields are among the most common form elements. They allow users to type in text, such as their name, email, or other information.

```html
<label for="name">Name:</label>

<input type="text" id="name" name="name">
```

Radio Buttons and Checkboxes

Radio buttons and checkboxes offer users choices in a list format. Radio buttons allow users to select a single option from a list, while checkboxes allow multiple selections.

```html
<label>Gender:</label>

<input type="radio" id="male" name="gender" value="male">

<label for="male">Male</label>

<input type="radio" id="female" name="gender" value="female">

<label for="female">Female</label>


<label>Hobbies:</label>

<input type="checkbox" id="reading" name="hobbies" value="reading">

<label for="reading">Reading</label>

<input type="checkbox" id="gaming" name="hobbies" value="gaming">

<label for="gaming">Gaming</label>
```

Select Dropdowns

Select dropdowns allow users to choose an option from a predefined list. The <option> element is used to define each choice within the dropdown.

```html
<label for="country">Country:</label>
<select id="country" name="country">
  <option value="usa">United States</option>
  <option value="canada">Canada</option>
  <option value="uk">United Kingdom</option>
</select>
```

Submit Button

Finally, the submit button serves as the trigger for users to submit the form. It's often used alongside other input elements.

```html
<input type="submit" value="Submit">
```

Form Validation and Security

Forms play a critical role in collecting accurate and secure data. HTML5 introduces attributes like required for mandatory fields and pattern for input validation. Additionally, server-side validation is crucial to ensure data integrity and security.

By harnessing the power of HTML forms, you'll be able to create interactive web experiences, gather user data, and engage your audience in a meaningful way.

Chapter 4: CSS Essentials

Welcome to the world of cascading style sheets! In this chapter, we'll delve into the captivating realm of CSS, where you'll learn to transform your web pages from mere structures into visually captivating experiences. From inline styles to external stylesheets, from selectors to properties, we'll equip you with the essential tools to wield the magic of CSS and create stunning designs.

4.1 Introduction to CSS

CSS, or Cascading Style Sheets, is the enchanting language that adds aesthetics and visual appeal to your web content. It's what allows you to turn the raw structure of HTML into a canvas of colors, typography, spacing, and layouts. Think of HTML as the skeleton and CSS as the clothing that gives it life and character.

When you visit a website, what initially captures your attention? It's the design—the colors that resonate with the brand's identity, the typography that sets the tone, the layout that guides your eye. All of these are meticulously crafted using CSS.

CSS empowers you to:

Define colors that resonate with your brand or theme. Imagine a travel website with a palette of soothing blues and greens that evoke the tranquility of oceans and forests.

Choose fonts that convey the right tone and readability. A fashion blog might use elegant serif fonts to match its sophisticated content, while a tech website might opt for clean and modern sans-serif fonts.

Create layouts that guide users through your content seamlessly. CSS enables you to position elements precisely, ensuring that your content flows naturally and is easy to navigate.

Add decorative elements like borders, shadows, and gradients. A call-to-action button can stand out with a subtle drop shadow, while a testimonial section might have a gradient background for added depth.

CSS operates on the principle of cascading. This means that styles can be inherited from parent elements to their children. If you set a font size on a parent container, its child elements will inherit that size unless otherwise specified. This cascading nature simplifies the process of styling multiple elements consistently.

As you journey further into CSS, remember that while it adds beauty and elegance to your web pages, it's also a tool for enhancing usability. Clear typography, sufficient contrast between text and background, and responsive layouts contribute to an optimal user experience.

In the upcoming sections, we'll explore various aspects of CSS in detail. You'll learn how to apply styles to text, backgrounds, and other elements, and you'll gain insight into the world of selectors and properties. By the end of this chapter, you'll have a solid foundation in CSS, ready to bring your design visions to life.

4.2 Inline, Internal, and External CSS

CSS offers you multiple ways to apply styles to your HTML elements. Each method has its own advantages and use cases. Let's explore the three primary methods: inline, internal, and external CSS.

Inline CSS allows you to apply styles directly to specific HTML elements using the style attribute. While this method provides immediate and specific styling, it's most suitable for quick adjustments rather than extensive styling. For instance:

```
<p style="color: blue;">This is a blue paragraph.</p>
```

Internal CSS resides within the <style> element in the HTML document's <head> section. It's a step toward separation of concerns, as it keeps the styles separate from the HTML content. This approach allows you to define styles for multiple elements without cluttering the HTML tags themselves.

```
<head>
   <style>
     p {
        color: green;
     }
   </style>
</head>
<body>
   <p>This is a green paragraph.</p>
</body>
```

External CSS is the recommended approach for maintaining clean and organized code, particularly as your project grows. With external CSS, you create a separate .css file and link it to your HTML using the <link> element. This promotes a clear separation between content and presentation, making your code easier to manage.

```
<head>
  <link rel="stylesheet" type="text/css" href="styles.css">
</head>
```

External CSS also has the advantage of allowing styles to be cached by browsers, leading to faster loading times for repeat visitors. It encourages modularity, enabling you to reuse styles across multiple pages.

As your projects become more complex, external CSS becomes increasingly valuable. It fosters maintainability, consistency, and efficient collaboration among developers and designers. When changes are required, you can update styles in a single location—the external stylesheet— effectively propagating those changes to all connected HTML pages.

In the next sections, we'll delve deeper into the art of selectors and properties. These fundamental concepts will empower you to target specific elements and define the visual rules that govern their appearance. By mastering these concepts, you'll have the keys to shaping the design of your web pages.

Stay tuned for the continuation of Chapter 4, where we'll explore the art of selectors and properties, revealing how you can shape the appearance of your web content with precision.

4.3 Selectors and Properties

In the world of CSS, selectors and properties form the foundation of design customization. Selectors allow you to target specific HTML elements, while properties define the visual attributes that you want to apply to those elements. Let's dive into these concepts and discover the magic of crafting stunning designs.

Understanding Selectors

Selectors are like the keys that unlock the doors to specific HTML elements. They enable you to pinpoint elements you want to style. Here are some common types of selectors:

Type Selectors: Target elements based on their HTML tag name. For instance, p targets all paragraphs, and h1 targets all level-one headings.

Class Selectors: Use classes to group elements and style them uniformly. A class selector is denoted by a period (.) followed by the class name. For example, .highlight targets all elements with the class "highlight."

ID Selectors: IDs provide a unique identifier for an element. An ID selector is denoted by a hash (#) followed by the ID name. For instance, #header targets the element with the ID "header."

Attribute Selectors: These target elements with specific attributes. For example, [type="submit"] targets all elements with the attribute type set to "submit."

Defining Properties

Properties are the directives that determine the appearance of targeted elements. Each property is paired with a value that specifies how the element should look. Here are some common properties and their usage:

color: Changes the text color. For instance, color: red; sets the text color to red.

font-family: Specifies the font type. font-family: Arial, sans-serif; selects Arial as the preferred font, followed by a generic sans-serif font in case Arial isn't available.

font-size: Adjusts the font size. font-size: 16px; sets the font size to 16 pixels.

margin: Defines space outside the element's borders. margin: 10px; adds 10 pixels of margin on all sides.

padding: Sets space inside the element's borders. padding: 5px; includes 5 pixels of padding on all sides.

By combining selectors and properties, you have the ability to craft intricate and visually appealing designs. For example, consider the following CSS code:

```css
/* Style all paragraphs with class 'info' */
p.info {
    color: #333;
    font-size: 14px;
    padding: 10px;
    border: 1px solid #ccc;
```

```
}
```

In this example, the class selector .info targets all paragraphs with the class "info." The properties applied define the text color, font size, padding, and border. This creates a cohesive and visually pleasing design for informative paragraphs.

The Cascade and Specificity

The term "cascading" in CSS refers to the order of styles applied when multiple rules target the same element. If there's a conflict between styles, the cascade resolves it based on specificity and source order. Specificity refers to the weight of a selector. For example, an ID selector (#header) has higher specificity than a class selector (.header), and a class selector has higher specificity than a type selector (h1).

If two conflicting rules target the same element, the one with higher specificity takes precedence. If specificity is equal, the rule that appears later in the stylesheet wins. Understanding specificity is essential to predict how styles will be applied when you have complex CSS.

4.4 Applying Styles to Text and Backgrounds

With a solid grasp of selectors and properties, let's delve into applying styles to specific aspects of your web content. Text and backgrounds are two fundamental components of design that CSS empowers you to customize effectively.

Text Styling

Text plays a crucial role in conveying information and evoking emotions. CSS grants you the power to adjust various aspects of text to align with your design vision. Here are some key text properties and their usage:

color: Set the color of the text. For instance, color: #FFD700; changes the text color to a vibrant gold.

font-family: Specify the font for your text. font-family: 'Helvetica', sans-serif; selects the font "Helvetica" and falls back to a generic sans-serif font if it's not available.

font-size: Control the size of your text. font-size: 18px; sets the font size to 18 pixels.

font-weight: Adjust the thickness of the text. font-weight: bold; makes the text bold.

These properties, among others, allow you to create text that's not only visually appealing but also legible and accessible to users.

Background Styling

Backgrounds set the mood for your content and contribute significantly to the overall user experience. CSS provides you with a plethora of options to customize backgrounds:

background-color: Change the background color of an element. For example, background-color: #f2f2f2; sets a light gray background.

background-image: Add an image to the background. background-image: url('background.jpg'); sets "background.jpg" as the background image.

background-size: Control how the background image is sized. background-size: cover; scales the image to cover the entire element.

By thoughtfully combining text and background styling, you create a harmonious and visually engaging design that captures your audience's attention and guides them through your content seamlessly.

With a firm understanding of selectors, properties, and styling principles, you're ready to embark on a journey of creativity. In the upcoming sections, we'll delve deeper into advanced styling techniques. We'll explore the magic of colors, gradients, typography, borders, and shadows. Stay tuned as we unlock the full potential of CSS to craft immersive and captivating web experiences.

Chapter 5: Styling with CSS

Welcome to the captivating realm of CSS styling! In this chapter, we'll embark on a journey of design transformation, where you'll learn to harness the power of CSS to craft visually stunning web pages. From the foundational concepts of the box model to the interplay of colors, gradients, typography, borders, and shadows, you'll unlock the secrets that elevate your content from ordinary to extraordinary.

5.1 Box Model: Margin, Padding, Border

In the world of web design, the box model is a cornerstone concept that shapes how elements are structured and spaced within a layout. Imagine each HTML element as a box, with distinct layers that define its space, appearance, and separation from neighboring elements.

Margin: The outermost layer of the box, margin creates space around an element, establishing a visual buffer between elements. It prevents content from feeling cramped and contributes to a balanced and well-structured design. Margins are transparent areas that don't have any background color or content.

Padding: Nestled within the margin, padding defines the space between an element's content and its border. It ensures that content has room to breathe and prevents it from touching the border. Padding enhances readability and provides a visual cushion that improves the overall aesthetics.

Border: Encircling the padding, the border outlines the boundary of the element. It can be solid, dashed, or dotted, with varying thickness and colors. Borders not only define the visual limits of an element but also contribute to its overall style.

Consider the following CSS example:

```css
.box {
```

```css
    margin: 20px;

    padding: 30px;

    border: 2px solid #007BFF;

}
```

In this example, the .box class creates an element with a margin of 20 pixels, padding of 30 pixels, and a solid blue border. This combination of margin, padding, and border produces a well-defined and visually appealing box that effectively separates it from its surroundings.

Understanding the nuances of the box model is essential for creating layouts that are balanced, organized, and visually pleasing. By skillfully manipulating margins, paddings, and borders, you gain the ability to shape the spatial relationships between elements and create compelling designs that draw users in.

Stay tuned as we continue our journey through the art of CSS styling. In the upcoming sections, we'll explore the enchanting world of colors, gradients, typography, borders, and shadows, uncovering the techniques that breathe life into your web designs.

5.2 Working with Colors and Gradients

Colors are the brushstrokes that paint emotions and personality onto your web pages. CSS empowers you to wield a rich palette, infusing your designs with vibrancy and meaning.

Color Properties: CSS offers a spectrum of color properties. The color property defines the text color, while the background-color property sets the background color of an element.

```css
.header {

    color: #FF5733; /* Vivid orange text color */

    background-color: #F0F4C3; /* Soft pale yellow background */

}
```

Gradients: Gradients are the magical transitions between colors that add depth and intrigue to your designs. A linear gradient blends colors along a straight line, while a radial gradient radiates from a central point. This allows for smooth color transitions or even the creation of captivating patterns.

```css
.button {

  background-image: linear-gradient(to right, #FF5733,
#FFC300);

}
```

Gradients aren't limited to two colors; they can encompass multiple colors, creating captivating effects that captivate users and direct their attention.

Understanding the psychology of colors is also crucial. For instance, blue might evoke feelings of trust and serenity, while red could signify passion and urgency. By thoughtfully choosing colors and applying gradients, you'll resonate with your audience on a deeper level, conveying emotions and enhancing the overall user experience.

5.3 Typography: Fonts, Sizes, Spacing

Typography, the art of arranging and styling text, is a subtle yet powerful aspect of design. CSS grants you the ability to fine-tune fonts, sizes, and spacing, ensuring your content is both aesthetically pleasing and readable.

Font Properties: The font-family property allows you to choose the typeface for your text. You can select from a vast array of fonts, aligning your typography with your brand's personality or the mood of your content.

```css
body {

  font-family: 'Open Sans', sans-serif; /* Elegant font with fallback */

}
```

Font Size and Spacing: The font-size property determines the size of your text, contributing to the overall hierarchy of content. Additionally, properties like line-height and letter-spacing influence the spacing between lines and characters, respectively.

```css
p {

  font-size: 18px;

  line-height: 1.5;

  letter-spacing: 0.5px;

}
```

Typography isn't just about aesthetics; it plays a significant role in enhancing the user experience. Legible text with appropriate spacing ensures that readers can consume your content effortlessly, fostering engagement and comprehension.

As you journey deeper into the realm of CSS styling, you'll discover that the interplay of colors, gradients, typography, borders, and shadows forms the tapestry of design. In the forthcoming sections, we'll unveil the magic of adding borders and shadows, elevating your designs from flat to dimensional and from ordinary to extraordinary.

5.4 Adding Borders and Shadows

Welcome to the world of dimensionality and depth! Borders and shadows are the secret ingredients that transform flat elements into visually engaging components. In this section, we'll explore how CSS enables you to craft borders that frame your content and shadows that add realism and intrigue.

Border Properties: Borders define the edges of an element, providing structure and visual separation. CSS offers extensive control over borders, allowing you to specify thickness, style, and color.

```
.button {

   border: 2px solid #007BFF; /* Blue solid border */

}
```

You can also target individual sides of an element to create diverse effects:

```css
.card {

  border-top: 1px dashed #888; /* Dashed top border */

  border-bottom: 3px double #555; /* Double bottom border */

}
```

Box Shadow: Shadows bring an element to life by simulating light and perspective. The box-shadow property creates shadows that appear beneath or around an element. You can control the shadow's position, blur, spread, and color.

```css
.card {

  box-shadow: 0 4px 6px rgba(0, 0, 0, 0.1); /* Subtle box shadow */

}
```

The box-shadow property enables you to craft a range of effects, from subtle and elegant to bold and striking. By thoughtfully applying shadows, you add realism and depth to your designs, making elements pop off the screen.

Combining Borders and Shadows: Borders and shadows work harmoniously to create compelling visuals. For instance, combining a border and a shadow can make an element appear elevated and prominent:

```css
.button {

    border: 2px solid #007BFF; /* Blue solid border */

    box-shadow: 0 2px 4px rgba(0, 0, 0, 0.2); /* Subtle box shadow */

}
```

Through the strategic use of borders and shadows, you can manipulate depth perception and guide users' focus, making your content more engaging and interactive.

Congratulations! You've now explored the full spectrum of styling techniques that CSS offers. From the foundational concepts of the box model to the artistry of colors, gradients, typography, borders, and shadows, you're equipped with the tools to create visually captivating web designs.

But our journey doesn't end here. In the upcoming chapters, we'll delve even deeper into the intricacies of web development. We'll explore the process of structuring complete web pages, implementing interactivity, optimizing performance, and publishing your creations to the internet.

Prepare to take your skills to the next level as we venture into the realm of creating fully functional and visually stunning web experiences.

Chapter 6: Layout and Positioning

Welcome to the world of layout and positioning, where you'll unravel the mysteries of structuring web content and arranging elements on the screen. In this chapter, we'll explore the fundamental concepts that govern how elements interact with one another, including the versatile display properties, element positioning techniques, the art of responsive design using media queries, and the power of flexbox and grid layouts.

6.1 Display Properties: block, inline, inline-block

In the realm of web design, understanding how elements behave within the layout flow is akin to mastering the choreography of a dance. Display properties dictate how elements interact with each other, influencing their positioning, dimensions, and how they respond to various screen sizes. Let's dive deeper into the three key display properties: block, inline, and inline-block.

Block Elements: Elements with a display value of block are like solo performers on a stage. They create a clear boundary around themselves, pushing any neighboring elements to the above and below. Block elements stretch horizontally to fill the available width of their container.

Imagine a <div> element with a class of .section:

```css
<div class="section">This is a block-level element.</div>


.section {

   display: block;

   width: 100%; /* Fills the entire width */

}
```

Block elements are great for structuring content into distinct sections, such as headers, paragraphs, and dividers. They provide a clear visual separation between different pieces of content, making your layout organized and easy to understand.

Inline Elements: Inline elements are like words within a sentence—they flow within the text content. They don't introduce a new line and can sit beside other inline elements. This is useful for elements like links and spans.

```
<p>This is an <span class="emphasis">emphasis</span> inline element.</p>

.emphasis {

   display: inline;

   font-style: italic;

}
```

Inline elements are especially handy when you want to apply styles to individual portions of text without disrupting the natural flow of the content.

Inline-Block Elements: The inline-block value is like a versatile dancer—it combines the characteristics of both block and inline elements. An element with display: inline-block sits within the flow of text content, just like an inline element. However, it can also have dimensions specified using properties like width and height.

Consider a navigation menu:

```html
<ul class="menu">

    <li><a href="#">Home</a></li>

    <li><a href="#">About</a></li>

    <li><a href="#">Services</a></li>

</ul>


.menu li {

    display: inline-block;

    margin-right: 20px;

}
```

In this example, the list items are displayed inline-block, allowing them to form a horizontal menu. The margin-right property creates spacing between the items, enhancing readability.

Understanding and leveraging these display properties will elevate your ability to create layouts that are not only visually appealing but also adaptable to different screen sizes and devices. Whether you're building a blog, an e-commerce site, or a portfolio, mastering these display properties is essential for effective web design.

Stay tuned as we explore more dimensions of layout and positioning. We'll delve into positioning techniques that allow you to precisely control the placement of elements within your layout.

6.2 Positioning Elements: relative, absolute, fixed

Welcome to the art of element positioning—a symphony of precision that transforms a blank canvas into a visual masterpiece. Just as a painter meticulously arranges colors on a canvas, a web developer arranges elements on a screen. CSS provides three primary positioning techniques—relative, absolute, and fixed—each with its own set of rules and creative possibilities.

Relative Positioning: Think of position: relative as giving an element a sense of awareness of its original position within the layout flow. When an element is positioned relatively, you can nudge it from its default position using properties like top, right, bottom, and left.

Imagine a scenario where you want to create a navigation menu with icons beside the menu items:

```
<ul class="menu">
```

```html
    <li><a href="#"><i class="icon home"></i>
Home</a></li>
    <li><a href="#"><i class="icon about"></i>
About</a></li>
    <li><a href="#"><i class="icon services"></i>
Services</a></li>
</ul>
```

```css
.menu li {
    position: relative;
    padding-left: 30px;
}

.icon {
    position: absolute;
    top: 0;
    left: 0;
    width: 20px;
    height: 20px;
    /* Define icons' background images here */
}
```

In this example, each menu item has an icon positioned absolutely at the top-left corner. By combining relative and absolute positioning, you create a cohesive layout where icons enhance the visual experience without affecting the flow of the content.

Absolute Positioning: When an element has position: absolute, it's like giving it the freedom to escape the confines of its parent and position itself based on its nearest positioned ancestor. This technique is incredibly powerful for creating overlays, tooltips, and complex layout arrangements.

Consider a scenario where you want to create an image gallery with captions that appear on hover:

```
<div class="gallery">

    <img src="image1.jpg" alt="Image 1">

    <div class="caption">Beautiful sunset</div>

</div>


.gallery {

    position: relative;

}
```

```css
.caption {

    position: absolute;

    bottom: 0;

    left: 0;

    width: 100%;

    background-color: rgba(0, 0, 0, 0.7);

    color: white;

    padding: 5px;

    opacity: 0;

    transition: opacity 0.3s;

}


.gallery:hover .caption {

    opacity: 1;

}
```

In this example, the .caption div is positioned absolutely at the bottom of the .gallery container. The :hover pseudo-class is used to reveal the caption by changing its opacity. This creates an elegant hover effect that enhances the user experience.

Fixed Positioning: Elements with position: fixed are like anchors in a turbulent sea—they remain fixed in their position relative to the viewport, even as the user scrolls. This is often used for navigation bars or headers that should always remain visible.

```html
<header class="header">
  <!-- Header content here -->
</header>
css
Copy code
.header {
  position: fixed;
  top: 0;
  left: 0;
  width: 100%;
  background-color: #333;
  color: white;
  padding: 10px 20px;
  z-index: 1000;
}
```

In this example, the header is positioned fixed at the top of the viewport. The z-index property ensures that it remains above other elements in the layout.

By understanding and applying these positioning techniques, you gain the power to create dynamic and visually compelling layouts. Each technique offers unique advantages, and mastering their interplay allows you to craft intricate designs that captivate your audience.

Stay tuned for more insights into layout and positioning. In the upcoming sections, we'll explore the art of responsive design using media queries, and we'll unravel the magic of flexbox and grid layouts—techniques that revolutionize the way you approach layout design.

6.3 Creating Responsive Designs with Media Queries

In the ever-evolving landscape of web design, catering to a diverse range of devices and screen sizes is a non-negotiable imperative. This is where the magic of responsive design comes into play. With the advent of smartphones, tablets, laptops, and desktops, ensuring that your web pages look and function well across various platforms has become a fundamental skill.

What Are Media Queries?: Media queries are a fundamental building block of responsive design. They allow you to apply different styles based on the characteristics of the user's device, such as its screen width, height, orientation, and resolution. This enables you to create designs that adapt gracefully to different devices, ensuring a consistent and optimal user experience.

Defining Media Queries: Media queries are typically defined using the @media rule in your CSS. You specify a condition based on certain criteria, and if that condition is met, the associated styles are applied.

```css
/* Example of a media query for screens with a width of 768px or less */

@media (max-width: 768px) {

  .header {

    font-size: 16px;

  }

}
```

In this example, when the screen width is 768px or less, the font size of the .header element is adjusted to 16px. This ensures that the text remains legible on smaller screens.

Mobile-First vs. Desktop-First: When designing responsive layouts, you have two primary approaches: mobile-first and desktop-first. Mobile-first involves designing for smaller screens first and then using media queries to enhance the layout for larger screens. Desktop-first starts with a default desktop layout and uses media queries to adjust for smaller screens.

Mobile-first is often recommended because it encourages a streamlined and efficient design process. However, the choice depends on your project's requirements and audience.

Viewport Meta Tag: To ensure that your responsive design works as intended, include the viewport meta tag in the <head> of your HTML document. This tag tells the browser how to scale and size the content to fit the screen.

```
<meta name="viewport" content="width=device-width, initial-scale=1.0">
```

By embracing responsive design and leveraging the power of media queries, you create web experiences that cater to the user's device, whether it's a smartphone, tablet, laptop, or desktop. This approach enhances user satisfaction, reduces bounce rates, and ultimately contributes to the success of your website.

In the upcoming sections, we'll dive into the remarkable worlds of flexbox and grid layouts. These CSS techniques revolutionize the way you structure layouts, enabling you to create intricate designs with ease.

6.4 Flexbox and Grid Layouts

Enter the realm of layout design with a pair of CSS powerhouses—flexbox and grid layouts. These techniques are game-changers, offering unparalleled control over how elements are arranged within a layout. Whether you're building a simple navigation menu or a complex multi-column design, flexbox and grid provide a flexible and efficient approach to layout creation.

Flexbox Layout: Flexbox, short for "flexible box," is a one-dimensional layout model that excels at distributing space and aligning items within a container, even when the container's dimensions are unknown or dynamic.

Defining a Flex Container and Items: To create a flex layout, set the display property of the container to flex. This transforms the container's children into flex items, allowing you to control their alignment and distribution.

```css
.container {

    display: flex;

    justify-content: space-between;

    align-items: center;

}
```

In this example, the .container becomes a flex container with its child elements as flex items. The justify-content property spaces the items evenly across the container, and align-items centers them vertically.

Flex Direction and Wrapping: The flex-direction property determines the main axis along which flex items are laid out. The default is row, which arranges items horizontally. You can also use column to stack items vertically.

```css
.container {

    display: flex;
```

```
    flex-direction: column;

}
```

Adding flex-wrap: wrap allows items to wrap to a new line if they exceed the container's width. This is especially useful for creating responsive layouts.

Grid Layout: Grid layout is a two-dimensional layout system that enables you to create complex layouts with rows and columns. It's like a digital grid on which you can place items in precise locations.

Creating a Grid Container and Items: To establish a grid layout, set the display property of the container to grid. Then, define the rows and columns using properties like grid-template-rows and grid-template-columns.

```
.container {

    display: grid;

    grid-template-rows: 1fr 2fr;

    grid-template-columns: repeat(3, 1fr);

    gap: 10px;

}
```

In this example, the .container becomes a grid container with two rows and three columns. The 1fr and 2fr values distribute available space proportionally.

Grid Areas and Placement: You can define named grid areas using the grid-template-areas property. This makes it easy to place items within specific sections of the grid.

```css
.container {

    display: grid;

    grid-template-rows: 1fr 2fr;

    grid-template-columns: repeat(3, 1fr);

    gap: 10px;

    grid-template-areas:

        "header header header"

        "sidebar main main";

}


.header {

    grid-area: header;

}
```

```css
.sidebar {

  grid-area: sidebar;

}


.main {

  grid-area: main;

}
```

In this example, each item is assigned to a specific grid area using the grid-area property. The result is a structured and visually pleasing layout.

Flexbox and grid layouts offer unparalleled control over how elements are arranged within a layout. Whether you're designing a simple navigation bar, a card-based layout, or a complex multi-column design, these techniques provide the flexibility and power needed to create visually stunning and responsive layouts.

As we conclude our journey through layout and positioning, you're armed with the knowledge to craft layouts that adapt seamlessly to various screen sizes and orientations. In the subsequent chapters, we'll explore the process of creating complete web pages, adding interactivity, optimizing performance, and finally, publishing your creations to the internet.

Chapter 7: Creating a Complete Web Page

Welcome to the chapter where all the puzzle pieces come together. In this section, you'll learn the art of weaving HTML, CSS, and interactivity into a cohesive and engaging web page. From structuring your content to adding interactive animations, you're about to embark on a journey that culminates in the creation of a complete and dynamic digital experience.

7.1 Structuring a Web Page Using HTML5 Elements

Creating a compelling web page requires more than just slapping together a few lines of text and images. It involves crafting a thoughtful and well-organized structure that not only captures the essence of your content but also guides visitors seamlessly through your digital domain. In this section, we'll explore the art of structuring a web page using HTML5 elements—a skill that's essential for creating user-friendly, accessible, and search engine-friendly web experiences.

The Power of Semantic HTML5 Elements

HTML5 introduces a variety of semantic elements that provide meaning and context to different parts of your web page. Unlike the old days of using generic <div> elements for everything, these new elements allow you to convey the purpose and role of each section, making your code more readable and understandable for both humans and machines.

Creating the Header and Navigation

The <header> element takes the spotlight at the top of your web page, serving as the gateway to your content. This is where you introduce your brand, display a logo, and provide the primary navigation that guides visitors through your website. To make your navigation more accessible, wrap it in the <nav> element.

```
<header>

  <h1>Welcome to Travel Haven</h1>

  <nav>

    <ul>

       <li><a href="#home">Home</a></li>
```

```
      <li><a href="#about">About</a></li>

      <li><a href="#services">Services</a></li>

      <li><a href="#contact">Contact</a></li>

    </ul>

  </nav>

</header>
```

Structuring the Main Content

The <main> element is the heart of your web page, containing the most essential content that visitors came to see. Inside the <main> element, you can use different semantic elements to structure your content logically. For example, <article> can be used for self-contained pieces of content, while <section> can be employed to group related content together.

```
<main>

  <section id="about">

    <h2>About Us</h2>

    <p>Discover our journey and mission...</p>

  </section>

  <section id="services">
```

```
<h2>Our Services</h2>

<article>

    <h3>Web Design</h3>

    <p>Create stunning websites that...</p>

</article>

<article>

    <h3>SEO Optimization</h3>

    <p>Boost your online presence with...</p>

</article>

</section>

<!-- More sections go here -->

</main>
```

Crafting the Footer

The <footer> element marks the end of your web page and provides closure to the visitor's journey. It's a great place to include copyright information, links to social media profiles, and additional resources.

```
<footer>

    <p>&copy; 2023 Travel Haven. All rights reserved.</p>
```

```html
    <ul class="social-icons">

        <li><a href="#"><i class="fab fa-facebook"></i></a></li>

        <li><a href="#"><i class="fab fa-twitter"></i></a></li>

        <li><a href="#"><i class="fab fa-instagram"></i></a></li>

    </ul>
</footer>
```

The Benefits of Semantic Structure

By using these semantic HTML5 elements, you're not just adding a visual structure to your web page; you're creating a meaningful and organized experience for your visitors. Search engines also appreciate the clear hierarchy that these elements provide, potentially improving the visibility of your website in search results.

As you craft your web page's structure, remember that each element you use serves a specific purpose in guiding and engaging your audience. With a well-structured foundation in place, you're ready to move on to the exciting realm of styling and design.

7.2 Styling Your Page with CSS

With the structural framework of your web page established using HTML5, it's time to unleash your creativity and transform your content into a visually captivating masterpiece. Cascading Style Sheets (CSS) are your artistic tools, allowing you to wield colors, typography, spacing, and layout to craft a design that not only pleases the eye but also enhances the user experience.

Defining a Consistent Color Palette

Color is a powerful tool that evokes emotions and sets the tone for your website. Select a color palette that aligns with your brand and content. CSS variables, also known as custom properties, enable you to create a centralized color palette that can be easily adjusted across your styles.

```css
:root {

  --primary-color: #3498db;

  --secondary-color: #e74c3c;

  --background-color: #f2f2f2;

}
```

Typography Matters

Typography plays a crucial role in web design, influencing readability, user engagement, and the overall aesthetic. Choose fonts that resonate with your content's personality. CSS provides the font-family property to specify font choices and the font-size property to establish a consistent text size.

```
body {

    font-family: 'Open Sans', sans-serif;

    font-size: 16px;

}


h1, h2, h3 {

    font-family: 'Raleway', sans-serif;

}
```

Creating Layout Harmony

Your web page's layout is the canvas on which your content unfolds. Employ CSS techniques to structure your content and create a balanced design. Techniques such as margins, paddings, and the box model enable you to control spacing between elements and ensure a visually pleasing arrangement.

```css
.container {

  width: 80%;

  margin: 0 auto;

  padding: 20px;

  background-color: var(--background-color);

  box-shadow: 0 2px 4px rgba(0, 0, 0, 0.1);

}
```

Navigation Styling

Navigation menus are central to user experience. Elevate your navigation styling with CSS rules that make it easy for users to navigate your site. Consider using transitions to add smooth animations when users interact with navigation links.

```css
nav ul {

  list-style: none;

  display: flex;

  gap: 20px;
```

```css
}

nav a {
    text-decoration: none;
    color: var(--secondary-color);
    transition: color 0.3s;
}

nav a:hover {
    color: var(--primary-color);
}
```

Adding Depth with Shadows and Borders

Shadows and borders can add a sense of depth and separation to your elements, enhancing the overall visual appeal of your design. Use these properties judiciously to create a hierarchy of focus within your content.

```css
.card {
    background-color: white;
    padding: 20px;
```

```css
border-radius: 8px;

box-shadow: 0 2px 4px rgba(0, 0, 0, 0.1);

border: 1px solid #e0e0e0;

}
```

As you wield CSS to craft your web page's visual aesthetics, remember that each design choice should align with your content's goals and the user experience you aim to create. A well-executed design not only makes your website visually appealing but also reinforces your brand identity and encourages user engagement.

Stay tuned as we delve into the exciting realm of implementing navigation menus and breathing life into your design with CSS transitions and animations.

7.3 Implementing Navigation Menus

Navigation menus are the roadmap that guides visitors through your website's content. They provide users with a sense of orientation, helping them explore different sections of your site effortlessly. In this section, we'll delve into the art of implementing navigation menus using HTML and CSS, ensuring that users can navigate your content with clarity and ease.

Structuring the Navigation Bar

The navigation bar, often found at the top of the page, serves as the central hub for your navigation links. You can structure it using an unordered list <ul> and list items <li>, with each list item containing a link. By using semantic HTML5 elements, you're not only enhancing the accessibility of your navigation but also making it easier to style with CSS.

```html
<nav>
  <ul>
    <li><a href="#home">Home</a></li>
    <li><a href="#about">About</a></li>
    <li><a href="#services">Services</a></li>
    <li><a href="#portfolio">Portfolio</a></li>
    <li><a href="#contact">Contact</a></li>
  </ul>
</nav>
```

Creating Responsive Navigation

In the era of mobile devices, responsive design is paramount. As the screen size changes, your navigation menu should adapt to ensure a seamless user experience. One popular approach is to create a mobile-friendly "hamburger" menu that expands into a full menu when clicked.

```html
<nav>

  <input type="checkbox" id="menu-toggle">

  <label for="menu-toggle" class="menu-icon">

    <span></span>

    <span></span>

    <span></span>

  </label>

  <ul class="menu">

    <li><a href="#home">Home</a></li>

    <li><a href="#about">About</a></li>

    <!-- More menu items go here -->

  </ul>

</nav>
```

Styling the Navigation Menu

CSS transforms your navigation list into a polished and user-friendly menu. Use properties like display, padding, border, and background-color to create visually appealing links. When implementing a mobile menu, consider using CSS transitions to add smooth animations to the menu icon.

```css
nav ul {
    list-style: none;
    display: flex;
    gap: 20px;
}

nav a {
    text-decoration: none;
    color: var(--secondary-color);
    transition: color 0.3s;
}

nav a:hover {
    color: var(--primary-color);
}
```

Navigation Accessibility

Remember that accessibility is crucial for all users, including those with disabilities. Ensure that your navigation links are keyboard-friendly and provide clear visual cues. Use appropriate HTML attributes like aria-label to label navigation elements for screen readers.

```
<a href="#home" aria-label="Home">Home</a>
```

User-Friendly Navigation Transforms the Experience

By implementing navigation menus that are well-structured, responsive, and visually appealing, you create an enjoyable user experience that encourages visitors to explore your website further. Thoughtful navigation design ensures that users can easily access the information they're seeking, increasing the likelihood of engagement and conversion.

As you refine your navigation menus, prepare to infuse your design with interactive animations and transitions that elevate your web page's visual dynamism.

7.4 Adding Interactivity with CSS Transitions and Animations

A static web page is like a painting; it captures a moment frozen in time. But the web is a dynamic and interactive realm, and to truly engage your audience, you need to breathe life into your design. CSS transitions and animations are your tools to create movement, transformation, and interactivity that capture users' attention and enhance their browsing experience.

Understanding CSS Transitions

CSS transitions allow you to smoothly change property values over a specified duration, adding a touch of elegance to your design. Transitions are triggered by changes in an element's state, such as hovering over a link or clicking a button. The transition property, combined with other properties like color, background-color, and transform, can bring your design to life.

```css
button {

    background-color: var(--primary-color);

    color: white;

    padding: 10px 20px;
```

```css
  border: none;

  transition: background-color 0.3s ease-in-out;

}


button:hover {

  background-color: var(--secondary-color);

}
```

Animating Elements with Keyframes

CSS animations take interactivity to the next level by allowing you to create complex sequences of transitions. The @keyframes rule defines a set of keyframes that describe how an element should animate over time. You can control properties at different stages of the animation, such as from, to, or specific percentage points.

```css
@keyframes bounce {

  from {

    transform: translateY(0);

  }

  to {

    transform: translateY(-20px);
```

```css
    }

}

.button-animate {

    animation: bounce 0.5s infinite alternate;

}
```

Adding Hover Effects

Hover effects provide immediate visual feedback to users as they interact with elements on your web page. You can create hover effects by targeting elements with the :hover pseudo-class and applying changes to their properties.

```css
.card {

    background-color: white;

    padding: 20px;

    border-radius: 8px;

    box-shadow: 0 2px 4px rgba(0, 0, 0, 0.1);

    border: 1px solid #e0e0e0;

    transition: transform 0.3s ease-in-out;

}
```

```
.card:hover {
  transform: scale(1.05);
}
```

Designing with Purpose

While CSS transitions and animations offer exciting possibilities, remember that moderation is key. Interactivity should enhance the user experience, not overwhelm it. Use transitions and animations purposefully to draw attention to important elements, guide users' focus, and provide subtle visual cues.

Balancing Aesthetics and Performance

Although animations can be visually captivating, they can also impact page performance if used excessively. Be mindful of performance considerations, especially on devices with limited resources. Test your animations on various devices and browsers to ensure a smooth experience for all users.

By skillfully integrating CSS transitions and animations into your design, you create a dynamic and engaging experience that keeps visitors exploring your content with curiosity and delight.

With your web page now fully structured, styled, and enriched with interactivity, you're ready to optimize and prepare for its grand debut on the world wide web.

Chapter 8: Optimizing and Publishing

Congratulations! You've journeyed through the fascinating world of web development, from understanding the basics of HTML and CSS to crafting interactive web pages that captivate users. As you stand at the threshold of completing your web project, there are a few crucial steps remaining before your creation can truly shine on the digital stage. Chapter 8 is your guide to the final leg of your web development journey—optimizing and publishing your web page.

In this chapter, you'll dive into the art of performance optimization, ensuring that your web page loads swiftly, delivering a seamless and enjoyable user experience. You'll explore techniques to fine-tune your content, minimize load times, and enhance accessibility. Beyond optimization, you'll gain insights into testing your website across various browsers to ensure consistent functionality and appearance for all users. You'll also navigate the intricacies of choosing the right hosting solution and domain name, making strategic decisions that impact your website's accessibility and discoverability.

As you near the finish line, you'll embark on the exciting voyage of deploying your web page to the vast landscape of the internet. You'll learn the step-by-step process of making your creation accessible to users worldwide, sharing your passion, expertise, or products with the global online community.

Each section of this chapter is a stepping stone toward a polished and professional web presence. From optimizing performance to hosting considerations and the final deployment, you'll equip yourself with the knowledge and skills needed to confidently bring your web project to fruition. So, let's explore the intricacies of optimizing and publishing your web page, ensuring that it stands out amidst the digital expanse with speed, accessibility, and a memorable user experience.

8.1 Performance Optimization Tips

As you approach the final stages of bringing your web creation to life, one critical aspect demands your attention: performance optimization. In a fast-paced digital world, users have little patience for slow-loading websites. Ensuring that your web page is optimized for speed and efficiency not only improves user experience but also contributes to better search engine rankings. In this section, we'll explore essential performance optimization tips to make your web page lightning-fast.

Optimize Images

Images are often the heaviest assets on a web page. To prevent them from slowing down your website, use image compression tools to reduce file sizes without compromising quality. Formats like JPEG, PNG, and WebP offer different trade-offs between image quality and file size. Additionally, consider lazy loading images, which delays the loading of images until they come into the user's viewport.

```
<img src="image.jpg" alt="A beautiful landscape" loading="lazy">
```

Minify CSS and JavaScript

Minification involves removing unnecessary whitespace, comments, and reducing variable names in your CSS and JavaScript files. This makes your code more compact and efficient to load. You can use online tools or build processes to automate this process.

Use Browser Caching

Leverage browser caching to reduce load times for returning visitors. Set cache expiration headers on your server to instruct browsers to store certain files locally. This means that when a user revisits your site, the browser can fetch cached files instead of re-downloading them.

Utilize Content Delivery Networks (CDNs)

CDNs distribute your website's assets across multiple servers worldwide. When a user accesses your site, the assets are delivered from the server closest to their location. This minimizes latency and ensures faster load times, especially for users located far from your web server.

Prioritize Critical Above-the-Fold Content

Above-the-fold content refers to what users see without scrolling. Prioritize loading critical CSS and essential content for this area first. This approach, known as "critical rendering path optimization," ensures that users can quickly see and interact with your page while the rest of the content loads in the background.

Performance Testing

After implementing these optimization techniques, it's crucial to test your website's performance. Use tools like Google PageSpeed Insights, GTmetrix, or WebPageTest to analyze your website's load times, identify bottlenecks, and receive suggestions for improvement.

By implementing these performance optimization strategies, you're not only creating a faster and more efficient website but also demonstrating your commitment to providing a seamless user experience.

8.2 Testing Your Website Across Browsers

Creating a visually stunning and interactive web page is a remarkable achievement, but ensuring that it functions consistently across different web browsers is equally crucial. Browsers come in various flavors, each with its own rendering engine and interpretation of web standards. As a web developer, it's your responsibility to ensure that users have a seamless experience regardless of the browser they choose. In this section, we'll delve into the art of testing your website across browsers to achieve cross-browser compatibility.

Understanding Browser Differences

Browsers interpret HTML, CSS, and JavaScript differently, and these variations can lead to inconsistencies in how your web page is displayed and functions. What looks perfect in one browser might appear distorted or broken in another. It's essential to be aware of these differences and adopt best practices to address them.

Use Modern Web Standards

Modern web standards are designed to be interoperable across browsers. Favoring these standards over browser-specific features reduces the likelihood of compatibility issues. CSS Flexbox and CSS Grid, for instance, are well-supported layout techniques that offer consistent results across most modern browsers.

Choose Cross-Browser Compatible Libraries

When integrating third-party libraries or frameworks into your project, opt for those that prioritize cross-browser compatibility. Libraries like jQuery, Bootstrap, and Vue.js have dedicated teams that ensure their components work well across different browsers.

Implement Progressive Enhancement

Progressive enhancement is a design philosophy that ensures your website functions well on all browsers while providing enhanced experiences for browsers that support modern features. Start with a core experience that works on all browsers and gradually add advanced features for those using modern browsers.

Browser Testing Tools

Browser testing tools are invaluable allies in your quest for cross-browser compatibility. Here are a few tools that can help:

BrowserStack: A cloud-based platform that allows you to test your website on real browsers and devices.

CrossBrowserTesting: Offers a wide range of browsers, devices, and operating systems for testing.

Sauce Labs: Provides automated testing on a variety of browsers and devices.

Local Testing

While online testing tools are convenient, it's also important to perform local testing using different browsers available on your system. Install popular browsers like Google Chrome, Mozilla Firefox, Microsoft Edge, and Safari to observe how your website behaves on each.

User-Agent Switchers

User-agent switchers are browser extensions that allow you to emulate different browsers by changing the user-agent string. This can give you a sense of how your website appears to users on various browsers.

Emulators and Virtual Machines

Emulators and virtual machines are useful for testing your website on operating systems you might not have access to. Tools like VirtualBox and VMWare allow you to create virtual instances of different operating systems and browsers.

Regular Updates and Testing

Browsers evolve over time, and new versions are released regularly. It's important to stay updated with browser trends and test your website on the latest versions. Additionally, periodic testing ensures that any changes you make to your website don't inadvertently introduce compatibility issues.

By investing time and effort into testing your website across different browsers, you ensure that users have a consistent and delightful experience, regardless of the browser they prefer. Cross-browser compatibility is a testament to your dedication to delivering high-quality web experiences to a diverse audience.

8.3 Hosting and Domain Considerations

As your web page takes its final shape, it's time to address the critical choices of hosting and domain. These decisions not only impact the accessibility and performance of your website but also contribute to its overall branding and professionalism. In this section, we'll navigate the intricate landscape of hosting services and domain names, ensuring that your web page finds its rightful place on the internet.

Choosing a Hosting Provider

A hosting provider is your web page's home on the internet. It's where your files, databases, and assets are stored and served to visitors. When selecting a hosting provider, consider the following factors:

Types of Hosting: Shared hosting, VPS hosting, dedicated hosting, and cloud hosting offer different levels of resources and control. Choose a type that aligns with your website's needs and projected traffic.

Performance: Look for hosting providers with solid uptime guarantees and fast server response times. Performance is crucial for providing a seamless user experience.

Scalability: If your website is expected to grow in traffic, choose a hosting provider that allows easy scaling without disruptions.

Customer Support: Reliable customer support is essential for resolving technical issues and getting assistance when needed.

Security: Ensure the hosting provider offers security features like SSL certificates, firewall protection, and regular backups.

Registering a Domain Name

Your domain name is your website's online address, and it's a critical aspect of your brand identity. When selecting a domain name, keep these points in mind:

Relevance: Choose a domain name that reflects your website's purpose or content. It should give users a clear idea of what to expect when they visit.

Simplicity: Keep the domain name short, easy to spell, and free from hyphens or complicated characters. This makes it easier for users to remember and type.

Keywords: Including relevant keywords in your domain can help with search engine optimization (SEO).

Extension: The most common domain extension is .com, but consider other options like .net, .org, or country-specific extensions depending on your audience and purpose.

Mapping the Domain

Once you've registered a domain name and chosen a hosting provider, you'll need to map the domain to your hosting server. This involves updating your domain's DNS settings to point to the hosting provider's server.

Setting Up Email

Many hosting providers offer email services with your domain name. This adds a professional touch to your website and allows you to communicate with users using your domain-specific email address.

SSL Certificates

An SSL certificate is essential for securing data transmitted between your website and users' browsers. It also contributes to higher search engine rankings. Many hosting providers offer free SSL certificates through services like Let's Encrypt.

Migration and Backups

If you're migrating an existing website, ensure that the hosting provider offers migration assistance. Regular backups are crucial to prevent data loss in case of unexpected events.

Cost Considerations

Consider your budget when choosing a hosting provider and registering a domain. Balance cost with the features and performance you need for your website.

Review and Feedback

Before finalizing your hosting and domain choices, seek reviews and feedback from other users who have experience with the hosting provider or domain registrar. This can provide valuable insights into the quality of their services.

By carefully selecting a hosting provider and domain name that align with your website's goals, you set the stage for a professional online presence that's easily accessible to users around the world. Your choices influence not only the technical aspects but also the branding and reputation of your website.

8.4 Deploying Your Website to the Internet

With your web page fully optimized, thoroughly tested, and hosted on a reliable server, you're now ready to take the final step: deploying your creation to the vast expanse of the internet. Deploying a website involves making it accessible to users worldwide, turning your digital masterpiece from a local project into a global presence. In this section, we'll guide you through the process of deploying your website and making it live on the internet.

Uploading Files to the Server

Before your website can be accessed by users, its files must be uploaded to the hosting server. This can be done through various methods, including:

FTP (File Transfer Protocol): Use FTP clients like FileZilla to transfer files from your local machine to the server.

Git Deployment: If you're using version control with Git, you can set up automatic deployments to the server whenever you push changes to your Git repository.

Database Migration

If your website relies on a database to store content or user data, ensure that the database is set up and properly configured on the hosting server. You might need to export your local database and import it onto the server.

Domain Configuration

Ensure that your domain name is correctly mapped to the hosting server's IP address. This involves updating your domain's DNS records with the hosting provider's information.

Testing After Deployment

After deploying your website, thoroughly test it on the live server. Check for broken links, missing assets, and any issues that might have arisen during deployment.

Handling SSL Certificates

If you've set up an SSL certificate for your website, make sure it's properly configured on the live server. This ensures that your website is accessible over HTTPS, providing security to users' interactions.

Continuous Deployment

Consider setting up continuous deployment pipelines, especially if you plan to frequently update your website. Services like Jenkins or GitHub Actions can automate the deployment process whenever changes are pushed to your code repository.

Monitoring and Maintenance

Once your website is live, your journey doesn't end. Regularly monitor its performance, security, and user experience. Update content, fix any issues that arise, and keep an eye on server resources and traffic patterns.

Final Checks Before Launch

Before announcing your website to the world, conduct final checks:

Browser Testing: Ensure that your website works seamlessly across various browsers and devices.

Performance: Verify that your optimization efforts have paid off by testing load times.

Functionality: Double-check that all interactive elements, forms, and features work as intended.

Responsiveness: Confirm that your website responds well to different screen sizes.

Announcing Your Website

With your website live, it's time to share it with the world. Announce its launch on social media, through email newsletters, or any other channels relevant to your target audience.

Feedback and Iteration

After launching, pay attention to user feedback. Use analytics tools to gather insights into user behavior, page views, and interactions. Use this feedback to make iterative improvements to your website.

Celebrate Your Achievement

Deploying a website is a significant accomplishment. Take a moment to celebrate your hard work and dedication. Your creation is now accessible to a global audience, showcasing your skills and creativity.

By following these deployment steps and best practices, you ensure that your website is not only accessible but also functional, secure, and ready to make its mark in the online world.

Chapter 9: Next Steps in Web Development

As you've embarked on this exciting journey of learning about HTML and CSS, you've gained a strong foundation in crafting beautiful and functional web pages. However, the world of web development is vast and ever-evolving, offering endless opportunities for you to continue expanding your skills and creating more advanced and dynamic web experiences. In Chapter 9, we'll explore the next steps in your web development journey, diving into JavaScript, advanced CSS techniques, and the realm of building dynamic web applications.

9.1 Introduction to JavaScript

JavaScript is the dynamic force behind the modern web, propelling websites from static pages to interactive and responsive applications. As you delve into this powerful scripting language, you're unlocking the potential to create web experiences that engage users, validate forms, perform calculations, and even communicate with external data sources. This section will introduce you to the fundamentals of JavaScript, laying the groundwork for you to venture into more complex scripting and application development.

JavaScript: The Language of Interactivity

Imagine a web page that responds to user clicks, validates form inputs in real time, and updates content without requiring a page refresh. JavaScript is the magic that makes all of this possible. It's a versatile scripting language that runs directly in the browser, enabling you to create dynamic and interactive web applications. Whether you're aiming to build a simple calculator or a complex e-commerce platform, JavaScript is the tool you need to bring your ideas to life.

Variables and Data Types

At the heart of JavaScript are variables, containers that hold data. Variables allow you to store values such as numbers, strings, and objects, making them essential for manipulating and managing information within your scripts. JavaScript supports various data types, including:

Numbers: Integers and floating-point numbers for mathematical operations.

Strings: Textual data enclosed in single or double quotes.

Booleans: True or false values for logical comparisons.

Objects: Complex data structures that can hold properties and methods.

Arrays: Ordered collections of values, often used for lists of items.

Declaring a variable involves using the var, let, or const keywords, with let and const offering more modern and predictable behavior.

```
// Variable declaration using 'let'
```

```javascript
let age = 30;

// String variable
let name = "Alice";

// Boolean variable
let isStudent = true;

// Array variable
let colors = ["red", "blue", "green"];
```

Control Structures: Making Decisions and Loops

Control structures are essential for creating dynamic behavior in your scripts. Conditional statements, such as if and else, allow your script to make decisions based on certain conditions. For instance, you can display different messages depending on a user's input.

```javascript
let age = 18;

if (age >= 18) {
```

```javascript
  console.log("You are eligible to vote!");
} else {
  console.log("You are not eligible to vote yet.");
}
```

Loops, on the other hand, enable your script to repeat certain actions. The for loop is commonly used to iterate over arrays or perform a task a specific number of times.

```javascript
for (let i = 1; i <= 5; i++) {
  console.log("Iteration " + i);
}
```

Functions: Reusable Blocks of Code

Functions are the building blocks of JavaScript applications. They encapsulate a series of actions that can be executed whenever needed. Functions enhance the modularity and reusability of your code. You can define a function and then call it multiple times throughout your script.

```javascript
// Function to calculate the area of a rectangle
function calculateArea(width, height) {
```

```js
  return width * height;

}

let area = calculateArea(10, 5); // Call the function

console.log("Area:", area);
```

Document Object Model (DOM)

One of the most impactful aspects of JavaScript is its ability to manipulate the Document Object Model (DOM). The DOM represents the structure of a web page, and JavaScript allows you to dynamically change its content, structure, and styles. With DOM manipulation, you can create interactive elements, update text and images, and respond to user actions.

For instance, consider a button that toggles the visibility of a paragraph when clicked:

```html
// HTML: <button id="toggleButton">Toggle Paragraph</button>

//      <p id="targetParagraph">This is a hidden paragraph.</p>
```

```javascript
let toggleButton =
document.getElementById("toggleButton");

let targetParagraph =
document.getElementById("targetParagraph");


toggleButton.addEventListener("click", function () {

  if (targetParagraph.style.display === "none") {

    targetParagraph.style.display = "block";

  } else {

    targetParagraph.style.display = "none";

  }

});
```

Conclusion

As you've just scratched the surface of JavaScript, you've embarked on a journey of endless possibilities. JavaScript's versatility and ubiquity in web development enable you to create experiences that engage users and elevate your projects to new heights. In the subsequent sections of this chapter, you'll delve deeper into JavaScript, explore advanced CSS techniques, and even venture into the realm of building dynamic web applications. With JavaScript as your tool, you're equipped to craft web pages that not only look beautiful but also offer rich interactivity and user engagement.

9.2 Learning Resources and Further Reading

The field of web development is an ever-evolving landscape, where continuous learning is not just valuable—it's essential. In this section, we'll guide you through a curated selection of learning resources and further reading materials that will empower you to deepen your understanding, explore advanced concepts, and stay updated with the latest trends in web development.

Online Tutorials and Courses

Online tutorials and courses are a great way to learn web development at your own pace. They often include structured lessons, hands-on exercises, and quizzes to reinforce your learning. Some popular platforms for web development courses include:

Codecademy: Offers interactive coding lessons on HTML, CSS, JavaScript, and more.

freeCodeCamp: Provides a free and comprehensive curriculum covering a wide range of web development topics.

Coursera and edX: Platforms that partner with universities to offer both free and paid web development courses.

Books on Web Development

Books are timeless resources that offer in-depth explanations, real-world examples, and comprehensive coverage of web development topics. Some recommended books for expanding your knowledge include:

"Eloquent JavaScript" by Marijn Haverbeke: A comprehensive guide to JavaScript programming, suitable for both beginners and experienced developers.

"CSS Secrets" by Lea Verou: Dives into advanced CSS techniques and creative solutions for common design challenges.

"You Don't Know JS" by Kyle Simpson: A series of books that provide a deep dive into the nuances of JavaScript.

Coding Communities and Forums

Engaging with coding communities and forums is a great way to connect with fellow developers, ask questions, share knowledge, and stay up-to-date with industry trends. Some popular online communities include:

Stack Overflow: A question-and-answer platform where developers can ask and answer coding-related queries.

Dev.to: A community of developers sharing articles, tutorials, and insights on a wide range of web development topics.

Blogs and Newsletters

Blogs and newsletters are excellent resources for staying updated with the latest trends, best practices, and emerging technologies in web development. Some noteworthy sources include:

Dumi not Dummy: find nice tutorials and learning tips and tricks regarding programming.

CSS-Tricks: Offers tutorials, articles, and tips related to CSS and front-end development.

Smashing Magazine: Features articles on web design, development, and UX.

GitHub and Open Source Projects

GitHub is a treasure trove of open source projects, libraries, and frameworks that you can explore, learn from, and contribute to. By studying and contributing to open source projects, you'll gain valuable insights and collaborate with developers from around the world.

Advanced Web Development Topics

If you're looking to dive deeper into specific areas of web development, consider exploring these advanced topics:

Responsive Design: Master the art of designing web pages that adapt seamlessly to different screen sizes and devices.

Performance Optimization: Learn techniques to improve the speed and performance of your web pages.

User Experience (UX) Design: Explore principles and strategies for creating user-friendly and intuitive web interfaces.

Server-Side Programming: Venture into server-side technologies like Node.js, PHP, or Python to create dynamic web applications.

Online Coding Challenges and Competitions

Participating in coding challenges and competitions is an enjoyable way to test your skills and apply what you've learned in real-world scenarios. Websites like HackerRank, LeetCode, and Codeforces offer a variety of challenges that cover algorithms, data structures, and coding puzzles.

Attending Web Development Conferences

Consider attending web development conferences and meetups to connect with industry professionals, learn from experts, and gain insights into cutting-edge technologies. Conferences like CSS Dev Conf, An Event Apart, and Smashing Conf offer valuable networking and learning opportunities.

Conclusion

As you venture into advanced web development concepts, remember that learning is a continuous journey. Whether you're aiming to master JavaScript, explore advanced CSS techniques, or build dynamic web applications, these learning resources and reading materials are your companions on the path to becoming a proficient and innovative web developer. Stay curious, keep practicing, and embrace the opportunities to refine your skills and create exceptional web experiences.

9.3 Exploring Advanced CSS Techniques

While you've already delved into the basics of CSS, there's a rich world of advanced techniques that can take your web designs to the next level. In this section, we'll dive into some of these techniques, equipping you with the skills to create more complex, dynamic, and visually appealing styles for your web pages.

CSS Preprocessors: Enhancing Efficiency

CSS preprocessors like Sass (Syntactically Awesome Style Sheets) and Less introduce powerful features that simplify and enhance your CSS workflow. Preprocessors offer features like variables, nested selectors, and mixins, allowing you to write cleaner and more maintainable stylesheets.

Variables in Sass:

```scss
$primary-color: #3498db;

$secondary-color: #e74c3c;


.button {

  background-color: $primary-color;

  color: white;

}
```

```scss
.alert {

  background-color: $secondary-color;

  color: white;

}
```

Nesting and Mixins in Sass:

```scss
.container {

  width: 100%;

  padding: 20px;


  .section {

    background-color: lightgray;

    padding: 10px;

  }

}


@mixin button-style {

  background-color: $primary-color;

  color: white;

  padding: 10px 20px;
```

```scss
}

.button {
  @include button-style;
}
```

CSS Custom Properties (Variables)

CSS Custom Properties, also known as CSS Variables, introduce dynamic values that can be reused throughout your styles. They enhance the flexibility of your designs and make it easier to maintain consistent styling.

```css
:root {
  --primary-color: #3498db;
  --secondary-color: #e74c3c;
}

.button {
  background-color: var(--primary-color);
  color: white;
}
```

```css
.alert {

  background-color: var(--secondary-color);

  color: white;

}
```

CSS Animation and Transitions

Animating elements on your web page can add flair and interactivity. CSS offers animation and transition properties that allow you to create smooth and visually appealing effects.

```css
/* Using Keyframes for Animation */
@keyframes fadeIn {
  from {
    opacity: 0;
  }
  to {
    opacity: 1;
  }
}
```

```scss
.element {

  animation: fadeIn 1s ease-in-out;

}


/* Using Transitions */
.button {

  background-color: $primary-color;

  color: white;

  padding: 10px 20px;

  transition: background-color 0.3s ease-in-out;

}


.button:hover {

  background-color: $secondary-color;

}
```

CSS Grid and Flexbox

CSS Grid and Flexbox are layout systems that revolutionize the way you create responsive designs. CSS Grid offers a powerful grid-based layout while Flexbox provides flexible alignment and distribution of elements.

CSS Grid:

```css
.container {

  display: grid;

  grid-template-columns: repeat(3, 1fr);

  gap: 20px;

}


.item {

  background-color: lightgray;

  padding: 20px;

}
```

Flexbox:

```css
.container {

  display: flex;

  justify-content: space-between;

  align-items: center;
```

```css
}

.item {

  background-color: lightgray;

  padding: 20px;

}
```

Responsive Typography

Creating typography that looks great on all devices is a crucial aspect of web design. Using relative units like em, rem, and %, along with media queries, you can ensure that your text scales appropriately across different screen sizes.

```css
body {

  font-size: 16px;

}


h1 {

  font-size: 2em;

}
```

```css
@media (max-width: 768px) {

 body {

  font-size: 14px;

 }


 h1 {

  font-size: 1.5em;

 }

}
```

Conclusion

As you immerse yourself in these advanced CSS techniques, you're equipping yourself with the tools to create more sophisticated and visually captivating web designs. From CSS preprocessors and custom properties to animations, layouts, and typography, these techniques empower you to craft web pages that stand out, engage users, and deliver exceptional user experiences. The knowledge you've gained in this chapter will serve as a solid foundation as you venture into the exciting world of building dynamic web applications in the next section.

9.4 Building Dynamic Web Applications

Welcome to the pinnacle of your web development journey—building dynamic web applications. In this section, you'll explore the realm of interactive, data-driven, and user-focused web applications. By combining your HTML, CSS, and JavaScript skills, you'll craft experiences that respond to user actions, retrieve and display real-time data, and provide seamless interactivity.

Single-Page Applications (SPAs)

Single-Page Applications (SPAs) are a modern approach to web development that provides a smoother and more responsive user experience. SPAs load a single HTML page and dynamically update content as users interact with the application, eliminating the need for full page reloads.

Frameworks and libraries like React, Angular, and Vue.js empower you to build robust SPAs. They introduce concepts like components, state management, and virtual DOM manipulation, streamlining the process of creating complex user interfaces.

Fetching Data from APIs

Web applications often rely on external data sources to provide real-time information to users. APIs (Application Programming Interfaces) serve as bridges that allow your application to communicate with external servers and retrieve data. Using JavaScript, you can make HTTP requests to APIs and manipulate the received data.

```javascript
// Fetching data from an API using the Fetch API
fetch('https://api.example.com/data')
  .then(response => response.json())
  .then(data => {
    // Process and display the data
  });
```

State Management

As your web applications grow in complexity, managing the state (data) of your application becomes crucial. State management libraries like Redux (for React) and Vuex (for Vue.js) help you organize, update, and synchronize the data that drives your application's behavior.

User Authentication and Authorization

Building secure web applications involves implementing user authentication and authorization systems. By validating user credentials and managing user sessions, you can control access to certain parts of your application and protect sensitive data.

Real-Time Interactivity with WebSockets

WebSockets enable real-time communication between a web client and a server. They're ideal for applications that require instant updates, such as chat applications, collaborative tools, and live notifications.

```javascript
// Using WebSockets to establish a connection
const socket = new WebSocket('wss://server.example.com');

// Handling incoming messages from the server
socket.addEventListener('message', event => {
  const message = event.data;
  // Update UI with the received message
});
```

Deploying Web Applications

Once you've built your dynamic web application, it's time to deploy it to the internet. Cloud platforms like AWS, Heroku, and Netlify offer hosting services that make deployment straightforward. These platforms provide tools to manage domains, SSL certificates, and scaling to accommodate different levels of traffic.

Conclusion

As you venture into building dynamic web applications, you're reaching the pinnacle of your web development journey. By integrating HTML, CSS, and JavaScript in harmonious symphony, you're creating experiences that engage users, deliver real-time data, and respond to their actions with seamless interactivity. The skills you've gained throughout this book will empower you to not only create visually stunning web pages but also craft applications that solve real-world problems, enhance user experiences, and contribute to the ever-evolving landscape of the web.

Final word: Conclusions

Congratulations on completing your journey through "Crafting the Web: A Beginner's Guide to HTML and CSS Mastery"! As you reflect on the chapters you've explored and the concepts you've learned, take a moment to appreciate the incredible progress you've made. From understanding the basics of the web to building dynamic web applications, you've embarked on a transformative learning experience that has equipped you with essential skills in web development.

Reflecting on Your Learning Journey

Your journey began with an introduction to the captivating world of web development. You learned about the importance of HTML and CSS, laying the foundation for your exploration. Through each chapter, you delved deeper into these languages, discovering their intricacies and their role in shaping the digital landscape.

From structuring web pages and styling content to creating layouts and adding interactivity, you gained the expertise needed to craft web experiences that are both functional and visually appealing. Along the way, you explored advanced techniques, expanded your knowledge of JavaScript, and even ventured into building dynamic web applications.

Celebrating Your Achievements

Now is the time to celebrate your achievements. You've conquered the complexities of HTML and CSS, and you've harnessed the power of JavaScript to create interactive web pages. You've honed your skills in styling, layout design, and dynamic scripting, setting the stage for your future endeavors in web development.

As you look back on your journey, remember the projects you've completed, the challenges you've overcome, and the skills you've acquired. Each line of code you've written is a testament to your dedication and passion for this craft.

Encouragement for Future Growth in Web Development

As you conclude this book, consider it a stepping stone rather than a destination. Web development is a vast and continuously evolving field. New technologies, frameworks, and tools emerge regularly, offering exciting opportunities for growth and innovation.

Continue your learning journey by exploring advanced front-end and back-end development, diving deeper into JavaScript frameworks, and embracing emerging trends in web design. Engage with the web development community, attend conferences, participate in coding challenges, and collaborate on open source projects. Your growth in this field is boundless, and the possibilities are limited only by your curiosity and determination.

A Final Word

Whether you're building personal websites, contributing to larger projects, or pursuing a career in web development, the knowledge and skills you've gained from this book will serve as a solid foundation. As you navigate the ever-changing landscape of web technologies, always remember that learning is a continuous process. Embrace challenges, stay curious, and let your passion drive you to create exceptional web experiences that leave a lasting impact on users around the world.

Thank you for joining us on this journey through "Crafting the Web." Your commitment to mastering HTML, CSS, and JavaScript has empowered you to shape the digital world and bring your creative visions to life. Keep crafting, keep innovating, and keep pushing the boundaries of what's possible in web development. The web is yours to create and shape.

Appendices

In this appendix section, you'll find valuable resources that complement your learning journey in web development. These appendices provide quick access to important information, tools, and terminology that will enhance your understanding and proficiency.

Appendix A: Glossary of Key Terms

Web development comes with its own vocabulary, filled with technical terms and concepts. This glossary serves as a reference guide to help you navigate this terminology and grasp the meanings of key terms. From HTML and CSS to JavaScript and beyond, you'll find concise definitions that demystify the language of the web.

Appendix B: Quick Reference Guides for HTML and CSS Syntax

When you're deep in coding, having a quick reference guide at your fingertips can be invaluable. In this appendix, you'll discover concise reference sheets for HTML and CSS syntax. These sheets provide a snapshot of the most commonly used tags, attributes, and properties, making it easier to recall and apply them while building your web projects.

Appendix C: Recommended Tools and Software

A skilled craftsman needs the right tools to bring their visions to life, and web development is no different. In this appendix, you'll find a curated list of recommended tools and software that can enhance your coding experience, streamline your workflow, and empower you to create outstanding web pages and applications. From text editors to web browsers, version control systems to design software, this list covers a range of essential tools for every web developer's toolkit.

These appendices are designed to be your companions as you continue to explore, learn, and innovate in the world of web development. Use them as resources to enrich your knowledge, optimize your processes, and create exceptional web experiences that leave a lasting impact.